Contents

What are ants?

Ants are small **insects**. They have small bodies and six legs. Each leg has two small claws at the end.

4

Ants have two eyes, but they cannot see very well. They have **feelers** for touching and smelling.

feeler

eye

leg

claw

Most ants are black or brown.
Some ants are green.

Lots of ants live together in a nest.
In the nest are a few **queen** ants, some
male ants and many **workers**. The
queen and the male ants have wings
for part of their lives.

Big ants, like this one, are nearly as long as your little finger. They live in very hot countries. Most ants are much smaller.

queen ant

The **queen** ant is bigger than the **male** ants. The **workers** are the smallest ants.

How are ants born?

The young **queens** and **male** ants fly from the nest to **mate**. The male ants soon die and the queen ants start new nests. Their wings drop off.

10

The queen ant lays eggs in the soil.
A few days later, a baby **hatches** out
from each egg. It is called a **larva**.

eggs

cocoon

After about eight days each **larva**
makes a hard case round its body.
This is called a **cocoon**. Can you
see the one cocoon?

Inside the cocoon the larva turns into a young ant called a **pupa**. This takes three weeks. **Workers** cut open the cocoon to help the new ant out.

workers

cocoons

What do ants eat?

Ants like sweet things. They eat fruit and seeds. Ants also eat worms, caterpillars, and other **insects**.

14

Ants like to drink **honeydew**. They get this from greenflies. The ants stroke them with their **feelers**. Tiny drops of the dew come out.

greenfly

ant

Which animals eat ants?

Spiders, beetles, and some other **insects** eat ants.

Birds and frogs eat ants. In some countries, animals called anteaters eat ants.

How do ants move?

Ants move very fast. Some ants
follow each other in lines.

Ants use the **claws** on the end of their legs to help them climb. **Workers** do not fly. You might see **queen** ants and **males** flying in the summer.

19

Where do ants live?

Ants make their nests in places where they feel safe and warm. You can find them in old logs or under stones. Some ants build nests underground.

20

Ants make tunnels and little rooms
inside their nests.

21

How long do ants live?

queen

The **queen** ant can live for 10 or 15 years. She is safe in her special room. The **workers** protect her.

22

The **male** ants live for only a few months. Their work is done when they have **mated** with the **queen**. The **workers** live for about five years.

What do ants do?

Worker ants are very busy. They build
the nest and keep it tidy.

Workers lick the eggs to keep them clean. They collect food and feed the baby **larvae**. They also look after the **queen** and the **cocoons**.

How are ants special?

Ants live and work together.
They help each other.

Ants are small but they are very strong.

Thinking about ants

Look at this ants' nest. What jobs
do you think the ants are doing?

Here is part of a nest. Which are the **larvae** and which is the **cocoon**? Which stage comes first? What would you see when the cocoon breaks open?

Bug map

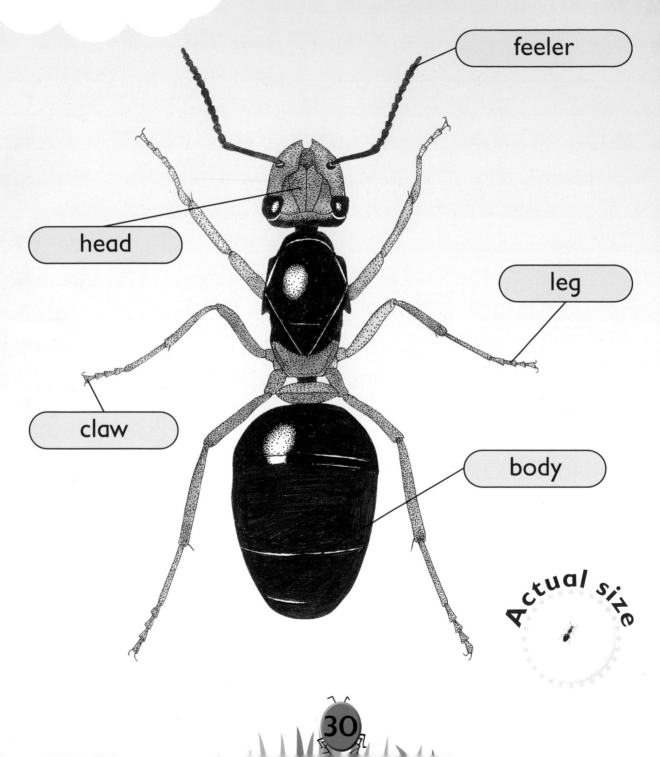

feeler

head

leg

claw

body

Actual size

30

Glossary

claws sharp, bent points at the end of the legs. Claws are used for tearing or holding things.

cocoon the case that grows round the larva

feelers two long thin tubes that stick out from the head of an insect. They are used to feel, smell or hear.

hatch to come out of an egg or cocoon

honeydew the sweet liquid made by greenflies

insect a small creature with six legs

larva (more than one = larvae) the little white grub that hatches from the egg

male a boy

mate when a male and female ant make baby ants

pupa (more than one = pupae) older larva

queen mother ant

workers ants that do all the work

Index

More books to read

Creepy Creatures: Ants, Sue Barraclough
(Heinemann Library, 2005)

32

Ant

Karen Hartley and Chris Macro

Heinemann LIBRARY

www.heinemann.co.uk/library
Visit our website to find out more information about Heinemann Library books.

To order:
☎ Phone 44 (0) 1865 888066
🖷 Send a fax to 44 (0) 1865 314091
🖥 Visit the Heinemann Bookshop at www.heinemann.co.uk/library to browse our catalogue and order online.

First published in Great Britain by Heinemann Library, Halley Court, Jordan Hill, Oxford OX2 8EJ, part of Harcourt Education.
Heinemann is a registered trademark of Harcourt Education Ltd.

Editorial: Clare Lewis and Katie Shepherd
Design: Ron Kamen, Michelle Lisseter and Bridge Creative Services Limited
Illustrations: Alan Fraser at Pennant Illustration
Picture Research: Maria Joannou
Production: Helen McCreath

Printed and bound in China by South China Printers

10 digit ISBN 0 431 01831 6
13 digit ISBN 978 0 431 01831 7
10 09 08 07 06
10 9 8 7 6 5 4 3 2 1

British Library Cataloguing in Publication Data
Hartley, Karen
Bug Books: Ant - 2nd Edition
595.7'96
A full catalogue record for this book is available from the British Library.

Acknowledgements
The publishers would like to thank the following for permission to reproduce photographs:
Alamy Images p.9 (Blickwinkel); Heather Angel p.26; Ardea London Ltd p.5 (J Mason), Bruce Coleman Ltd pp.6 (J Taylor), 10, 29 (K Taylor); Corbis p.18 (K Tweedy-Holmes); FLPA pp.4, 13 (M Thomas); Garden Matters pp.11 (P Goetgheluck), 12 (C Milkins); Getty Images/Stone p.27 (T Flach); Nature Photographers Ltd p.24 (N Callow); NHPA pp14, 15, 23 (N Callow), 22 (S Dalton), 16 (D Heuclin), 25 (E Janes), 19 (E Soder); Oxford Scientific Films pp.8 (K Atkinson), 17 (A Butler), 21 (C Milkins); Papilio Photographic p28; Premaphotos pp5, 20 (K Preston-Mafham).

Cover photograph reproduced with permission of Corbis (George B Diebold).

The publishers would like to thank Nancy Harris for her assistance in the preparation of this book.

Every effort has been made to contact copyright holders of any material reproduced in this book. Any omissions will be rectified in subsequent printings if notice is given to the publishers.

The paper used to print this book comes from sustainable resources.

Any words appearing in the text in bold, **like this**, are explained in the Glossary